I0511013

Get Out There and Get a Job... Dear

Helping Others

LAND THAT JOB-

With the HERO Method

By George Valentine

Dedication:

In special thanks, this book is dedicated to my beloved wife Karen - a great gift from God to my life. Putting up with the highs and lows of someone writing a book is a challenge and she is always up for a challenge.

Also thanks to one of history's greats, the Apostle Paul, who in his letter to the Roman church (Romans 5:1-5) states that suffering produces endurance; endurance creates character and character, hope. And Hope does not disappoint. Words to remember in the job hunt, eh?

Introduction:

Millions of people around the world face the frustrating challenges of finding employment complicated by trying the old, tired methods of job hunting. Through the HERO method, together we change the job hunter's perspective, the language used and help the hunter find new hope.

Your role is pivotal in these changes whether you are family, a friend or an employment counselor. Many people were brought up on books on how to shake an employer's hand, how to fill in 'cookie cutter' resumes and to use slick answers to interview questions. They may balk at seeing themselves differently and more assertively as the HERO Method empowers them to do just that.

The following book gives you as much support as possible to describe the HERO Method, answer some difficult questions and help them use the method to land that job!

First, you are helping individuals review what they have to offer potential employers through their work, volunteer and personal life experience. Any time someone gave them responsibility and they "did right by them" counts as an important part of understanding what they offer. The key to HERO Method is that nothing that is off-limits. Even something that the person may consider frivolous may spark a memory of something else or someone else who makes the ideas come forward.

Please, use phrases that encourage and try to deflect any difficulty by referring to their strengths instead of weaknesses.

How does HERO Method address an individual's challenges? Most books on job hunting ask the hunter to downplay them in the interview, referring them as "baggage". The HERO method looks at this the other way noting that the employer is hiring the person with the character to have overcome these problems and challenges.

Supplies you will need: A notebook, 2 pens, this book.   On to the Method...

Table of Contents:

HERO uniquely focuses on the four aspects of ANY job. You have a lot to offer employers and HERO helps you find hidden qualities. The fun part for the counselor is you get to introduce them to the job hunter.

Using exercises and worksheets, you help the hunter understand skills and how they relate to that future envisioned.

When an applicant meets an employer only one person's opinion will matter. How to stop thinking like a job hunter and more like the hiring manager.

4. Putting it into words: Ideas for the Hunt

Now we connect the dots of the hunter's attributes and the needs of the employer. You just have to have the right words.

5. Getting past frustration: Gaining strength for the Hunt

How to move forward toward the dreams the Hunter has through the days of job hunting.

"Workshops"

1: My HERO inventory

2: What I have to offer

3: Researching My top 4 prospects –
Their Point Of View

4: Connecting the dots

5: My deficits and what I can do

Exercises :

Knowing Myself: 1. Where to put my "But"
2. Teaching baseball to aliens   3. A Lesson from the
Babe 4. Bees can't fly

Connecting with the employer: 1. Sizzle versus
steak/ frosting versus cake 2. Your cheeseburger
voice   3. 3 Q's, stress Q's 4. The Janitor Game

Job Search pointers: 1. Making Your Own Bullseye
2. Learning from a Lumberjack. 3. Getting past the
bulldogs 4. Care and feeding of references.

Misc.: 1. Lesson from Lord Churchill. 2. Those who
think they can. 3. Stan and Bruno. 4. Appreciating
your spiritual side.

Chapter One

Using HERO To Help Others

Congrats on your generous plan to help others -
Now comes the hard part

You have one of the most gratifying and frustrating jobs today - **helping someone you know look for a job.**

There are so many books out there helping the job hunter, often with the same advice. They focus on what to wear and snappy answers to interview questions, they miss the point and they miss supporting the friend and counselor entirely. We **end that problem *right now.***

In the following pages of support, fun exercises you can customize for the job hunter and hope for the future, together we will *get rid of old and inefficient ideas and give new perspectives including:*

Like how to stop thinking like a job hunter.

Seeing hidden valuable skills the hunter does not see... yet.

How to connect what the employer needs to what is already inside the applicant.

- Help support you in the work you are doing

Ideas useful in the job hunt and other aspects of life

Building a Seed Packet Resume

Seeing themselves and their challenges in new ways.

Lets get to work!

1. What is HERO and how can it help job hunters? How can it help ME as a counselor?

- YOU help the job hunter see herself in a different way

The job hunter is a complex animal, much more than can fit on a resume. Through better appreciating life experience, a fuller understanding of the employer's needs and discovering a way to connect the two together you will make a huge difference in making the hunter successful instead of remaining unemployed.

Your role is helping the job hunter see a different person in the mirror. The first step is to lay out clearly the four central aspects of any job –

Heart   Energy   Re-learning skills and Owning the work that you do.

You will help them see HERO from their point of view first - what each person offers from work and personal experience then see HERO from the hiring manager's point of view and what each job needs.

HERO defined:

Heart: Can you appreciate the needs and expectations of another person? Can you work together with others toward a common goal? Can you appreciate another person's point of view to the community?

An individual grows in 'heart' by showing how he is able to get along well with others and face problems or stressors together – such as a single mother who helps with a Head Start program.

Energy: Can you find the strength within yourself to keep moving forward when you are physically or mentally tired? Will you put out extra effort, even when no one else is watching? Can you maintain focus on the job to be done as you need to?

Work and life challenges can show the energy an individual has -- from the returning veteran to the high school graduate who helped in the family or community.

Re-learn: Do you have the ability to learn what you need to know for the task at hand efficiently and effectively? Can you adapt to changes and learn that new material quickly?

Often problems require an individual to learn new ways quickly -- such as learning how to care for an elderly relative or a disabled child.

Owning what you do: Are you able to take responsibility for mistakes you make? Can you change and improve after taking criticism and direction?

The ability to handle stress also shows that a person owns her work and experiences – from ex-convicts to senior citizens.

Through the HERO Method, you are helping people see the positives and hidden valuable skills in the things learned through challenges faced.

But First, Thanks...

Before we get to the practice, I want to personally thank you for your service to others. Wanting a job, meeting employer after employer, all the while facing bills and well-meaning friends who say "haven't found a job yet, eh?" is one of the most frustrating times in life.

Through your compassion - and the HERO Method - you may be shortening that anxious time and giving real hope to the job hunter. Thank you for your service.

- Looking backwards: Taking Inventory.

Take a few minutes and help the job hunter through the Workshop 1.

This helps the individual take a good look at how work and life challenges have developed valuable though often hidden skills.

Please assist each person in filling out each question… it is the foundation of the HERO Method.

Workshop 1. My Inventory

List below the things you have done <u>outside of work and family</u> – clubs, sports, volunteering

First column: A title for what I did

Second column: Describe what I did (duties, actions)

Third column: What I gained from it (skills, experience)

Fourth column: Full range of my responsibilities

Now do the same for your <u>Work Experience</u>: List every example of when there was something I did where I was given responsibility and I "did right by someone else" (from babysitting to volunteering work.

First column: A title for what I did

Second column: Describe what I did (duties, actions)

Third column: What I gained from it (skills, experience)

Fourth column: Full range of my responsibilities

Education and Training: Things I learned to be good (proficient) at, whether in school, at a job or in meeting personal and family needs.

First Column: Area of learning

Second Column: Benefit to me

Third Column: What I did with the learning

Fourth Column: How I know I am good at it

Keep the results of *Workshop 1* aside but available for later review. Now we move on to exercises to add some fun to the serious work of job hunting.

Often people are hesitant to express themselves positively because of a sense that no matter their hard work, they will not build that new future. The true problem is that they have their "but" in the wrong place.

As the person entrusted to help in building that new future, here is an exercise to help set things right.

Exercise 1.

The Most Essential Step:

Where to Put Your But

One of the greatest first steps in job hunting is learning where you put your but. (That is with one t in but... this is a family oriented book after all.) Stop for a second and listen to that internal conversation every job hunter has –

This is where the real battle for success is won or lost.

How do you face the ongoing fight between your goals and your challenges?

"I really want that job ... **but...**

I have this problem."

Or do you say to yourself

"I have this problem ...**but** ...

I really want that job."

In facing this question, it does not matter if your problem is big and impersonal or small and really personal, placing your but in the way of success stops you before you even get started.

Think about that for a moment.

It is very easy to watch the news and decide that times are too tough and how are you ever going to make it in times like these? THAT emotion will show itself in your walk, in the way you talk and will sap the energy in your smile and your style.

You aren't looking for twenty jobs, you are only looking for one person smart enough to see the energy and spirit inside of YOU and hire YOU. Lose that spirit because of something outside your power to change things and it will show up and have energy slowly leak out of your smile.

Now in the micro side of things you take a look at yourself in the mirror and do not like what you see. Yes, I would like that job but I am just too darned (fill in the blank) to get hired. Folks, when you say this to yourself you have just fired yourself before you even had a chance to get hired.

You are much more than your shortcomings – you are a valuable person and could become the employer's valued team member **if they could see past the problem**, right? Well, first YOU have to see past the problem to seeing you as part of that team. As the job hunter **THAT** picture in your mind is the most powerful thing you have going for you. Use it, do not lose it.

How you phrase the 'but' question determines your ultimate success. If your but comes *before* your 'problem', the last thing you think of is why you will NOT get the job. You have built a mountain to climb even before you get to the employer. **Whew!** Isn't it harder to go into the interview that way?

Putting the 'but' after the problem puts your desire and drive first. This shows self confidence that you are master of your fate, a problem solver and not just blown around by the winds of change around you.

Hey, think of these things from the employer's point of view, **who would you hire**?

Remember that the person with the self-*confidence to land the job despite barriers* is the employee who will solve problems at work with ease and confidence as well.

Making It Work:

Write down all of the things that are in your way in your job hunt, listing them as macro and especially the micro things affecting your hopes for your future work.

Make it a long list **(15 or more)** and include some

silly things like how it is bound to rain on workdays and you may get Darth Vader for a boss as well as personal things like I am pretty old or I have this prison record. Be honest and true to yourself.

Which ones of these are on the right hand of the 'but' sentence and which ones are on the left side? Be painfully honest with yourself because this IS all about you after all and if you are not honest you are only cheating yourself.

Sit back for a moment and take a look at the sentences where the problem stifles your chance for getting the job. Your tough chore here is to change your perspective on these issues to saying Yes, I have that problem, but I still want the job more.

You have now completed the easy part, we are just beginning our look into what the hunter is capable of.

Most people can express most of their HERO attributes such as getting along with people, showing examples of energy or the conscientiousness of "owning" what they do. Talking of strength in re-learning is often a hard one for people. How can they show ability in learning job aspects for the employer feels comfortable in the individual?

A way for many people to gain self-undestanding that they can learn is simple but requires first that you are out of this world. I mean it... for a few moments you are an alien from another planet in this one. Here is what I mean...

Teaching Martians About (Baseball)

In explaining HERO, many people get worried or humble. They say, "I'm not smart at all, **how can I tell the employer I have the brains for that job**... I will never get hired; I should just go home and eat worms". I reply "Stop! Worms?" followed by "if you do not know that you have the brains for the job, you are already as good as fired for a job you have never even applied for."

Here is a quick way to have the confidence that you have the brains in something you enjoyed learning or had to learn in order to survive.

Making It Work:

Pretend that a Martian has come to earth and says to you in your native language "hey, tell me about this *baseball* you earthlings have." (Or maybe it says "tell me about this thing called makeup" or "tell me some things about music, eh?")

Quickly, earthling, write 12 things you know about baseball (famous players, some of the rules, etc.), makeup (brand names, where/how applied, etc.) or music (styles, singers, instruments, etc.).

OK? Now write down twelve more (the survival of our planet depends on it, folks.)

Now finally add five more.

Now you have one impressed Martian in front of you saying "WOW! You know a lot about baseball/ makeup/ music...

you must do that for a living."

The two morals of this story are that

- if you can learn that much about something **that does NOT pay the rent**... think of how you will make yourself learn about things (like operating a cash register, learning a computer program, caring for elderly patients) **when it IS for money to pay the rent**.

- **It is already inside you**, folks. If you can talk baseball with an alien you can talk about yourself with anyone who today is a stranger and tomorrow may become your employer.

Now we move onto another part of the Workshop, where the hunter reviews in detail what HERO qualities she has. The important point here is that not only can the person SAY she can do things, she can back it up with real life examples.

Remember, the four essentials as follows:

H: Heart for the job:

- What can the applicant show proving she can understand and address the concerns and expectations of the clients?

Can she get along with others to meet the goals of the job?

E: Energy to meet the position's needs:

Employers look for that special unteachable quality of 'drive' and energy when it is not necessary, but deeply valued.

Can you show that the applicant has "drive"?

R: Ability to Re-learn:

Can this individual effectively and efficiently learn the skills and procedures for the job and adapt to the changes which are bound to come? How quickly can the applicant be trained so the supervisor can walk away knowing the job will be done right?

What proof from personal experience can the applicant provide?

O: Does the applicant OWN the work that gets done?:

How can the employer know that this person will have maturity and willingness to learn from inevitable mistakes?

Can you show this person taking on responsibility?

Know himself/put it into words/learn employer needs/connecting the dots

As a valued counselor, the first step is to understand the importance of each aspect of HERO and help the applicant how she fits in each essential category.

Ready? Remember that every job that ever was or ever will be has these four aspects. Helping connect the dots between an employer's needs and the applicant's qualities in each is where you come in.

The next step is to help the Hunter put into words what your HERO qualities are.

Workshop 2. My HERO qualities:

HEART: Work and life experience.

In column 1: Where I was:

In second column: People I worked with or helped:

In third column: Objective of that work:

People I served: Who they were/are (characteristics – what is a common theme among the people who were clients?)

:_____

What were/are they expecting from you? (the client's objectives and perspectives):

_____

Was/Is the relationship to the client variable from person to person? Give examples.

_____

Co Workers:

Who they are (experience, education, job description):

_____

What are **they** expecting from **you** (getting along, independent thought, etc.)

_____

Is there stress/tension expected in your relationship (how to handle that):

_____

Stakeholders of the employer: People who have a 'stake' in the operation of the employer – neighbors, media, etc.

Who are they? (Describe):

_____

What do they expect from you?

_____

Can you see the world from their POV?

_____

General Issues:

Now we begin to see the world from a new employer's point of view. Select a prospective employer of interest to the job hunter and review THESE questions.

For each employer, review these questions.

Employer Point Of View:

Customers:

What kinds of problems or conflicts can you expect to have on the job?

_____

Have you dealt with these kinds of conflicts or problems before and how well did you do with them?

_____

Co Workers:

What kinds of problems or conflicts can you expect to have on the job?

_____

Have you dealt with these kinds of conflicts or problems before and how well did you do with them?

_____

Stakeholders:

What kinds of problems or conflicts can you expect to have on the job?

_____

Have you dealt with these kinds of conflicts or problems before and how well did you do with them?

_____

ENERGY: Work and life experience.

In the first column:

Where I was/ my role in the work:

In the second column:

Examples of energy needed

In the third column:

Objective of that work/ outcomes:

Energy:

Here we continue focusing on a new job and the challenges ahead.

Employer Point Of View:

I want someone who faces challenges head-on.

Give examples of how/when you worked to resolve 3 tough problems:

_____

_____

I want someone who has worked hard when it was not expected, like overtime, or on a team practicing in the rain, something like that. Give me two examples of this you have done.

Everyone "hits the wall" and cannot work any further. Give an example of what it takes to exhaust you (this shows you understand your limitations):

I like people who volunteer and help out when they do not have to. Give me two examples of your doing this.

RE-LEARNING: Work and life experience.

Re-learning is the ability of the individual to learn something efficiently and effectively so that they can be trusted to do it right.

In column one:

Name of position held

In column 2:

What I had to know to do the job

In column 3:

How quickly did I learn/ adapt

In column 4:

Special aspects (did I train others, etc.)

Employer Point Of View:

Training is one of the hardest parts of doing the job - things are always changing - and everyone says they can learn. Give three examples of something you had to learn well quickly and well.

_____

How did you KNOW you learned it, what gave you the understanding that 'yes, I have learned it well'?

_____

I need people who can adapt to change. Tell me three times when you adapted well the changes at work or school or life?

_____

Owning It: Work and life experience.

This section refers to taking responsibility for work by being conscientious, improving through the constructive criticism of others and being honest. This often is the hardest one part of HERO to put into action with the employer but also one of the most important.

First, review your work and personal history as it relates to Owning It. First go over the times you met stressful situations and came out stronger.

In the first column:

Description of experience

In the second column:

What made it hard/ stressful?

In the third column:

Specifics about the experience

In the fourth column:

How did you learn from it?

Employer Point Of View:

I want to find someone from this pile of applications who will make mistakes - everybody makes mistakes - then learn from them.

Give me examples of times you have messed up and later learned from the mistakes:

_____

It is rare to find people who welcome a challenge and are willing to say "yes, that one is for me." It is part drive, part learning from mistakes but all about being truthful with me instead of a lie. Give me 2 examples of you doing the right thing when taking another road is available:

Now you can help 'connect the dots' in the remainder of the job hunt.

The beauty of the HERO Method is that now you can make those connections both in the mind of the job hunter, in her resumes, JIST cards or in interview preparation - but that will come later.

Before taking the step into better understanding the employer's point of view, let us focus on the Hunter's viewpoint toward himself and building a positive image of the future. We start with a lesson from Babe Ruth.

The Sad, Sweet Truth About George Herman Ruth

In his time, George "Babe" Ruth was one of the greatest and one of the worst ballplayers in the USA. For generations he held the record for most home runs -- many remember pictures of him standing alongside home plate *watching yet another shot fly over the outfield wall.*

There are also pictures of Babe walking back to the dugout after just striking out... again. You see the "Sultan of Swat" was the *greatest striker-outer* of his era, too.

Think about that for a moment. The Babe *could have* walked around with a mental picture of himself booming homers and had great confidence every time he played. He could also have pictured himself remembering the hundreds of times he would walk sadly, slinking back to the dugout after striking out, **again**.

It is all just a matter of perspective.

In job hunting you face some of the things the Babe felt. Throughout the hunt you face both **disappointment** and you some levels of ***success*** (hey, you knew enough to get this book, right?).

It is all up to you and how you look at yourself in the mirror. Remembering your homerun is a *whole lot more fun,* more satisfying and gives you more energy than dragging your feet and keeping the picture in your mind of striking out again. When meeting an employer, picture yourself cracking a home run. It'll show in your stride.

Tom Edison, inventor of the incandescent light bulb, tried & failed **over 2000 times** to put together what later was one of history's greatest inventions. Asked what he learned from months and months lost time and failures, he said "I learned 2000 ways **not** to make a light bulb."
It's all about *perspective.*

Making It Work:

Take a moment and draw *two pictures of yourself.* In the first draw a picture showing you *doing something you have accomplished* (*learned, did, or met an important duty*). Now write a caption describing the picture and what you are thinking at the time.

Under that draw a picture of you accomplishing something **you want to be doing someday**. Now write a caption about how you are feeling about doing that someday soon.

Hey, **HAVE SOME FUN** & draw the pictures. It's OK to erase and rewrite, ***but please have some fun.*** Make them things you will enjoy remembering in the days ahead when you hit home runs and make the occasional strike out. Remember that **your life is** an unfinished 'picture' with many miles to go and lessons to learn.

Picture #1

Picture #2

One more example a hunter may relate to as a reminder about appreciating what you have inside already.

'A Diamond is just a piece of coal that did well under pressure'

You never really know about a person – especially their character – until you have seen them handle pressure. It is only then that you see if the person remains a lowly piece of coal or becomes the diamond that lies inside. Remember that a diamond is just a piece of coal that did well under pressure.

The more you are able to present your courage and character – the ability to work well under pressure, work just as well on good days as bad – the more you are able to show your diamond-like qualities. But first YOU have to see it.

Making It Work:

List challenges you have faced in four sections.

A – In your studies. Academic counselors say it is not the super high school student who does well in college, but one who knows how to handle it when she cannot understand something easily and works hard to get it all learned.

B – In dealing with or helping others. How do you handle clients/customers who are difficult to deal with?

C – In the decisions to do the right thing, especially when what is right is not easy.

D – In dealing with your own personal challenges.

Let your mind drift through some divergent thinking searching the ways you have become the person you are. And remember that courage and conscientiousness are not all about brave actions...

it is often just a small voice inside telling you to keep going.

- Is there anything facing you now that challenges you to move from a piece of coal to a diamond?

- If you are facing challenges in the four sections noted above – how are you planning to address them now?

Now write down the answers to the above questions to show not just yourself but the stranger who will one day become your next employer.

- Not seeing self as a "job hunter" but as a solution to an employer's needs.

When two people come to the traditional job interview only one person's opinion really matters - the hiring manager. No matter how many people are in the meeting, the only view point that will count at the end of the meeting is the employer's.

How do you help the job hunter knowing the other person's point of view (POV) is the one that rules the day? Teach them NOT to think like a hunter, but like the job provider. It is like preparing for a test by thinking like what is important to the teacher.

As part of the preparation for the application and resume, think of what is important from the employer's POV and THIS is where the HERO Method can help no matter the job.

Every job has specific needs in the Heart, Energy, ability to Re-Learn and to Own the job qualities the employer is looking for. By seeing the job through those eyes, the hunter can prepare a better understanding of what she brings to the interview and better yet, how to express that connection.

- HERO Method helps in researaching job, seeing employer's POV

Have the Hunter use Workshop 2 to map out employer's concerns. This will be your guide to finding the matches between what the applicant brings and what the employer needs.

Applicants will need to research and appreciate the job from the hiring manager's POV. Help that job hunter come up with complete answers to the four aspects so she can piece by piece understand how her hidden skills meet the demands of the new job.

- HERO Method helps in writing new parts of the resume and interview prep

In the next chapter we focus on the hunter being able to

present differently to the employer. Get a current resume and application to a specific employer. Set it aside so we can compare it to the HERO materials.

A resume is a very personal item and you have both worked hard on it no doubt. The HERO resume will offer the opportunity to present all of what the hunter has to offer the employer in a new way with new words. Just enjoy the work together.

- The HERO Method helps the hunter understand the job more fully

You will also help the hunter see the world from the employer's perspective and gain an understanding that:

- what the hunter has that the employer needs

- how to express it

- and also where the hunter needs to build skills and qualifications for the future.

For now, please review the following questions with the hunter to make sure he understands each point:

Review:

Before we move forward, please review with the Hunter the four main aspects of HERO and what they mean.

Heart: Heart? What is involved in this one?

Seeing the world from someone else's perspectives and understanding their expectations.

What are different examples of heart? Give examples of your "heart" in work, volunteering, life.

Energy:

Looking at it from the employer point of view you would like to work for how do you define energy?

You can tell a lot about a person by how they handle adversity. What are three examples of how you have done that?

Relearn:

What did you learn from the "aliens and baseball" exercise? List three examples of something you had to learn quickly and you did.

What can I do now to show my interest, knowledge in the field I want to go into?

Learning really shows interest in their field.

Own It:

How do you show that you take responsibility for the work you do?

Give three examples of how you made a mistake and learned from it. Explain why accepting blame is not a sign of weakness.

First, let us help the hunter see herself in a new way and the way the individual knows **how to adapt** when facing a challenge.

In order to discuss adapting we turn to a story about bees. Here is an exercise that helps the individual see how she adapted and THAT is a valuable skill.

Bees Can't Fly: The real birds & bees story.

For generations physicists had proven that **bees can't possibly fly**. Such round, tubby creatures with those itty-bitty wings can't physically or aero-dynamically fly. But they do.

The theory went that if somehow we could get word to the bees that they cannot possibly fly and they should just stop trying, then millions of bees would suddenly fall out of the sky never to fly again.

Just a few years ago through slow motion photography, scientists found that if bees flapped their wings up and down they could not fly - but instead bees use a wavy motion **and only because**

they have adjusted or adapted, they <u>**CAN**</u> fly.

Ask the hunter:
"Did you ever hear that there are things you can't do because you are too short, fat, old, dumb, poor or just too <u>(fill-in-the-blank)</u>?"

Other people may say the same sad things over & over to you or worse yet maybe you are saying them to yourself. Repeating these lies about who you are and what you are capable of can limit you so that you may never "fly" to where you are capable of. *How about you?* What are ways you have adapted or adjusted to meet the challenges you have faced?

Making it Work:

- List 5 stories you know of where "everyone" thought something would happen and it did not? It does not matter where the story comes from – politics, sports, weather.
- Name 3 stories you have heard affecting people who broke through their supposed limitations.

- Finally, write down 3 things you have heard about your limits.

In each case, how did you adapt and change to beat the challenges you face?

Remember: *"Every great idea that ever was started with someone dreaming it and a thousand other people saying 'Are you crazy?"*

Beating Labels that are intended to Limit

Think about it for a moment and build a list of how the ability to adapt helps the hunter and in turn builds the skills needed in employment.

People who have lived with "labels" can now see themselves in a new mirror by using the HERO Method to consider what has been seen as a deficit instead now seen as valuable.

- "Disabled": To survive as someone who has a handicapping condition, you need to learn many things others do not about yourself, your community and how to resolve problems day to day. Whether learning about new medications, dealing with new care providers or accomplishing daily tasks a different way, you have to adapt to stresses as they arise in ways most people never learn.

Your skills in learning, dealing with many people and solving problems in changing ways are all valuable skills you bring to your next employer.

- **"Single parent"**: Instead of thinking of a single parent as a harried person with family stresses, think of how he handles those pressures. This pers on knows that when a child needs help with a late night earache, he alone has to solve the problem. He deals with so many people - from sitters to transportation to doctors to teachers and has to work well and maintain relationships with each of them.

Handling emergencies; being the one person in charge; dealing well with a broad variety of people and their different agendas - these are valuable skills for many jobs though these skills do not fit easily onto a resume. You have to KNOW you have these inside of you and with this knowledge see the world a little differently than you did before.

- **Military Veteran:** All hidden skills in HERO are found in the veteran. Each service member can detail the ability to work seamlessly as part of a team and the ability to appreciate the needs and perspectives of her supervisor. Every day she brings energy and drive even under stress.

Intangibles such as learning new skills efficiently and effectively and owning the work you have done despite inevitable mistakes makes the veteran a special job applicant.

- Ex-convict: Often someone who has "paid their debt to society" can show that in the time incarcerated the individual has examined himself fully and is willing to take responsibility for actions.

There are avenues for expunging the record, forgiving the offense or bonding the individual for the future. Whatever the ex-con job hunter does, she needs to show how she is living proof that the future is different from her past.

- "Too old": Few generations in history have adapted as quickly and completely to change in the world around them as today's elderly. Adjusting with communication technology from rotary phones to I-phones, they learn as they go - a great attribute on the job.

When the hunter can show how as an individual he has adapted to change, he will not just "talk" of being adaptable but also show the ability to "walk the walk" of facing challenges.

- Seeing the positives in life experience as valuable assets

As noted above, another part of the Bee exercise is helping the hunter's understanding the ability to adapt and to move forward through a challenge. The hunter learns through time to find strength in herself and this is something valuable to an employer often lost in traditional job hunting methods.

College recruiters, coaches and employers - all sorts of people who size up a person's performance - do not necessarily focus on what comes easy to a person but how they react to life when it is NOT easy.

Do you shrink away from a challenge or find that the problem is someone else's fault? Do you move forward and embrace things as an opportunity for change?

Think it through and get ready for the eye rolling exercise to challenge you on this quality.

Love that eye rolling

This is my favorite because unprepared applicants fall for it *every time*.

You are the employer for a moment... you have a job that requires a *go-getter attitude* and ability to do things and adapt to change. You want to avoid anyone who would utter the words "**I'm not going to do THAT**".

What to do? **Use an eye roller!**

Most of the time the eye-roller is a job related test sprung on the applicant at the right moment.

Once you have completed the interview and the applicant has begun to relax you notice his guard, up for most of the meeting, is relaxed now. NOW you may see the real person behind the well-rehearsed mask some wear at an interview when you **_HIT HIM WITH THE EYEROLLER_**!

As the employer, you give him a job related test, simple math for cashiers, a written test with vocabulary the right candidate should know. _THEN LOOK AT HIS EYES AND EXPRESSION!_   Did his eyes roll backwards and did he _sigh an 'oh, **not a test!' sigh?**_

If that is the case, the applicant just told the employer how he may deal with the **unexpected**. Hiring managers, always on the lookout for seeing past a mask the applicant may have to their actual personality may see the eye-rolling as seeing past a 'front'.

The application may have just lost a chance at landing this job today. Why hire the *eye-roller* when another candidate may enthusiastically grab the exam and welcome the test as a way to show skills?

When an employer springs an eye-roller such as
- a job related test
- says "come with me on a tour" or
- "I'll bring in another interviewer now"

welcome it and **<u>avoid</u>** the *eye roller expression* that can ruin a good interview in one second.

Making It Work:

What are some unexpected things that can be thrown at you in an interview? **Make a list of 4 strange questions** (like 'name six people living or dead you would invite to dinner tonight?' what animal most resembles you?) **or job related questions** (what would you do in unusual situations at work) **tests that can be dropped in front of an applicant.**

Ask a friend to give you an interview, have them select a few from your list or come up with their own and remember their thoughts to your reactions. Remember, the eyes have it, eh?

Whether dealing with unexpected questions or self-doubts, the Hunter needs to find courage from within. Here is an exercise to help in this matter.

<u>Courage – a small voice</u>

Sometimes you feel small as you search for someone smart enough to hire you. More and more you face the idea that your future will never look different from the present, slogging through more days like the day before.

The winner in the job search is often the person who projects a positive image – how to do that when the days are all so gray? Remember that sometimes courage is not about bravado, but is a small voice that says "well, I will try again tomorrow".

<u>Making It Work:</u>

Find three sayings for your motivation. Ask around to friends or look into it yourself – but make certain that these nuggets have meaning to you.

Make a list of people you know and respect – family, friends, teachers. What makes them unique and special in your estimation?

Now take these things that are special to you and write them down – say them loudly when you feel your spirits waning. Write down what makes people you respect special and read them as well.

Part of re-evaluating yourself and building a positive sense of the person within is seeing challenges as room for growth in becoming a more valuable applicant.

- See HERO deficits as room for improvement and growth

After the hunter sees how his HERO attributes describe that what is offered is of value, take a look at the other side. EVERYONE has deficits in their profile that would benefit from polishing up.

Before detailing how to appreciate and address the deficits, let us first review an attitude some face where they see their limitations as something that is a part that will not ever leave. The challenges they face will haunt them from now on... or until you teach them about Lord Winston Churchill.

"Lord Churchill - YOU are DRUNK"

Lord Winston Churchill had a quick wit that helped him in one famous encounter that helps with your job hunting: One night he was at a dinner filled with the richest, snootiest people in London.

One woman was shocked to see Lord Churchill had too much to drink. She shouted at him **"Lord Churchill, you are drunk!"**

Winston turned to her and said softly but directly **"Madame, tonight I am drunk and you are ugly. Tomorrow, I will be sober but you, sadly, will still be ugly."**

The lesson here is that **time and effort**, painful as they may be at the time, **can cure some temporary problems – but ugly stays on.**
Churchill would become clear and sober again, but her 'problem' would remain. How about you?

Making It Work:

List the aspects of yourself that are problems for you today and be true to yourself –
- Are you a slob?
- Do you have trouble taking orders or correction?
- Do you get into arguments too quickly?

Make another list of lessons you need in order to address the problems you face. What are the things that time and effort can get it done for you?

You have the opportunity to promote a way of seeing self and the world differently than the Hunter sees it today - even better than changing where they put the BUT in his life. Thanks, Mrs. Ashe...

Those who think they can

She was a single mom in the Great Depression, a time when there were not many supports for families in her situation. She began making and selling soap she would make in her bathtub with the little money she could put together.

Well, she got pretty good at selling and **with hope, hard work** and the help of others she created one of the largest cosmetics companies in the world and named it after herself, Mary Kay Ashe.

She regularly stated that one of the keys to her success is a phrase she never forgot:

"Those who think they can, can.

Those who think they cannot are right."

The point here is that it is essential you think you can accomplish something in order to finally do it.

People who question if they can are no less competent, smart or capable of meeting the goal. What holds them back is that they deep down do not think that they can make it. Think of the successful people you have heard of, met or read about. They all shared Mary Kay's secret.

Making It Work:

Review the HERO qualities the hunter has. You are still in the process of growing your HERO skills.

These are the sides of **who you are**… not someone else, not some model from another job hunting book but YOU.

Write your answers to the "Where's Your But?" exercise putting your goals at the end of every sentence. Then write Mark Kay Ashe's statement below them. Remember **"those who think they can, can, those who think they cannot are right. I think I can."**

You have the opportunity to help the hunter see their future differently in another way - seeing personal deficits as something he can change in the view of the four aspects of the HERO Method.

- Expanding your role: Teaching more fully the employer POV

Most job hunting books emphasize shaping the individual in small ways - a jazzier resume, bolder dressing to impress, sharper answers to interview questions. The HERO Method offers a different challenge to the hunter and to you, the counselor: Understand the employer's point of view and concerns in filling the job.

By appreciating the employer's needs, the hunter can 'connect the dots' and see herself as supplying what the job needs. By seeing the world with new eyes, the hunter not only sees herself as having hidden attributes but also as now seeing job hunting from the employer's viewpoint.

Now, onto looking at the hunt up-close.

Chapter 3.

Researching the Job

- New eyes looking at the top job hunting options

How can you see the world from the POV of the employer? How to focus research and improve the best opportunity to land that job? You help the hunter best by using the HERO method in understanding main aspects of jobs that are sought.

When a candidate goes into the job application process thinking only of the POV of the hunter...

- what can I say to show off my skills?

- what clothes make the strongest impression?

- when I shake hands, how to best grip the hiring manager's hand?

... he misses the point. Remember, at the end of the job hiring process, only one person's opinion matters... the hiring manager. By **appreciating the employer's POV** in detail, the hunter can adjust how he presents himself addressing the four essential aspects of any job, Heart, Energy, Re-Learning and Owning one's work.

The next step is helping the Hunter complete Workshop 3 for each of her top 4 prospective employers -

Workshop 3. The top four job prospects:

Listing the top four jobs I am hunting: (Repeated for each job)

First Job: Name of employer

_____

Name of job title I am hunting

_____

Heart:

As the employer, I need to know you will appreciate the needs and expectations of my clients. When you join my team, will you fit in or cause more trouble and make me regret hiring you?

The **clients or consumers** I will be dealing with in the job, what are they like?

_____

What do they want me to do for them/what do they expect of me in my new job?

_____

What is an example of a difficult situation I may be in with clients and how would I handle that?

_____

Co-workers: How do they interact with each other and what will they expect from me?

_____

Do we work together toward a goal or more individually? Do we face deadlines/pressure?

_____

What is an example of a difficult situation I may be in with my coworkers - how to solve it?

_____

Give 3 examples of the co-workers and management points of view in situations at work?

_____

Stakeholders: Name three of them and describe how would I interact with them?

_____

Energy:

Every job requires a level of energy - can you work as hard on days when it is sunny and you feel good as on rainy days when you wish you were home?

On a 'good day' at work, what are the physical and emotional challenges I will face?

_____

On a 'bad day' at work, what are the physical and emotional challenges I will face?

_____

Re-learning:

I need to know that you can learn the work of the new job effectively and efficiently so I can walk away knowing the job will be done well. Can YOU do THAT?

What will I have to learn to meet the responsibilities of the job well? (Are they about dealing with "things" like numbers or machines or people?)

_____

Does the job require being quickness in doing the job well? Give three examples:

_____

Is there frequent training as systems change? Can I adjust?

_____

How will I know I have learned the job well and can do it effectively and efficiently?

_____

Owning the Job:

As the employer, I need to know that people will be

responsible for the work they do, good and bad. I need to know you will defend my company and its consumers the best you can.

Give three examples of being able to accept and learn from correction and criticism.

_____

Employers care for the quality of work completed. Give three examples of meeting responsibilities you have had and meeting another's expectations.

_____

In detail, what describe the worst parts of the new job. How will you handle it?

_____

You will need to defend our reputation to our clients. Can you handle the requirements of confidentiality and consistent customer service related to this job?

_____

- **Connecting with the employer**

Now that the hunter can picture what the employer needs in qualities for the job, the Hunter needs to understand the day to day concerns the employer has. With limited time and the need to find people who have an investment in doing the job well, the hiring manager has other concerns the hunter needs to appreciate.

If you have the opportunity, you may want to show them the videos on "Valentine's Diner" wherein I pose as the owner of a diner for a lighthearted way of showing the point of view of the employer in hiring decisions.

Always end with a period:
www.youtube.com/watch?v=UFtC0K2ybIs

"Nothing Personal":
www.youtube.com/watch?v=iBOgGr-lZ04

Where to put your "But":
www.youtube.com/watch?v=T6qrZ2LBLIc

The difference between "Frosting and Cake":
www.youtube.com/watch?v=hrEUs0cG_uQ

Using your cheeseburger voice:
www.youtube.com/watch?v=vvDGaLSh_So

One way to step forward in this is to learn to use your Cheeseburger voice.

Using Your Cheeseburger Voice:

One great question each hunter needs to answer before hunting is *how to talk with a prospective employer* while making a first impression.

Your tone of voice needs to portray **assertiveness** and self-assurance. Your voice should not sound pushy or boastful; be polite and respectful, but not too soft-spoken. You need to be quick and show you understand the employer's time is valuable, but not too quick. In short, a voice blended like a fine wine (not a whine). *HOW ARE YOU SUPPOSED TO GET IT RIGHT?*

First of all, do not buy expensive job hunting books or hire speech coaches hoping that you hit *just the right sound* when talking to the employer.
Its already inside of you.

Quick! Raise your hand if you have ever ordered a cheeseburger (or soyburger for our vegetarian friends). *THERE!* THAT is the tone of voice you need! That commanding yet friendly tone is what you are hungering for. *Relax,* picture yourself ready to order and **say out loud** '*I want a cheeseburger.*" WOW! Say it again, slowly: "*I want a cheeeeseburrrger.*"

Hey, you really **mean it**! You said it straight, plain and seriously. **Sounds like you aren't leaving this place without that *cheeseburger*.** YOU *are not making excuses or apologies for what you want* to say. You are not bragging or angry, just direct.

Get the right tone in talking with the employer - use your *cheeseburger* voice from saying hello to getting through the interview:

- it's sensitive without being *whiney*
- it gets your **point across** easily
- it doesn't *frighten* or put-off employers
- its a well-known and accepted tone

The cheeseburger voice helps you in other areas. For now, practice it & enjoy it. With relish.

Making It Work:

Practice this tone of voice. Try saying other things you will be saying with that tone, like "I want to see the employer" or "I have the experience you are looking for." Make a list of 10 statements you will want to say to the employer and other statements you want to make to friends/teachers/coaches then practice them with that cheeseburger voice of yours.

Frosting and cake

My late grandfather used to warn me about seeing past a salesman's sweet words or the mirage of beauty on the outside when he warned me about people who are *"all frosting and no cake"*.

Employers watch out for that also looking past a hunter's glossy image that does not tell the employer about any substance or 'cake' beneath it.

Employers are careful not to be fooled by an applicant who is all sweet with nothing backing up what they actually did or can do in the future.

Sometimes the words have some meaning, but are not related to what THAT employer is looking for. Make certain you can give some cake after all. *How to do that?*

First, review your resume, application and answers to the HERO Worksheets **showing the cake**. Add more detail in specifics of what you can do – have proof with statistics, references who will back up the sweet sounding statements you make.

Second, the cake should be inviting to your audience – review the words about your accomplishments as related to THEIR interests (shows that you have found in the HERO research.) If the employers want angel food, avoid giving them devil's food.

Third, too much frosting makes the employer wonder how deep you have piled on that frosting. **Avoid too much sweetness** by underlining the fluff in your resume and other application materials - where can you cut back?

Making It Work:

Review your resume, applications and JIST card in and make the changes as needed. JIST cards are bulleted points of your best qualities/qualifications targeting what the employer is looking for.

Index IV: *Connecting the Dots:*

Putting it into words

Through the HERO Method, your role in the job hunt is partly helping the Hunter become motivated and more self-assured and partly helping her in understanding the employer's point of view and putting that knowledge into practice.

The final ingredient is learning how to put into words the connection between what the employer needs and what the Hunter can provide. The three main resources a job hunter has are resumes, applications and JIST cards. Here are ways to put these to the best use.

Here you can help the hunter put the connections into effective words. Here are some strategies:

Applications:

As you know, all an application needs to do is

1. get the employers attention, not get set aside into the pile of also-rans and

2. get the Hunter the opportunity for an interview.

Before writing anything on the application, look it over - this is the canvas you have the opportunity to paint your portrait on. Practice a bit and write five bullets indicating how your work and life experience meet what the employer needs. Write them down then check before writing on the application answer two questions

- does it use words appropriate to that employer?

- does it take into account the employer's point of view using HERO?

JIST:

JIST Cards are index sized cards which give job hunters the opportunity to put their qualifications together in short sentences or bullets form to highlight to the hiring manager why employing them is such a good idea.

The trick here is to focus on the wording the employer would appreciate. Make a rough draft from the study you have done regarding how your HERO skills relate to specific jobs.

Make certain you know the name, title and address of the hiring manager; write a cover letter then assemble one or two JIST cards specific to the job you are applying for and mail the person who can bring you closer to your dream.

Resume:

In building resumes which are specific to each prospective employer, the HERO Method gives the Hunter an opportunity to add personal experience as well as work history to the vitae.

By first approaching the resume from the employer's point of view and the HERO attributes she is looking for, the resume often writes itself. Make a list of the individual's Heart, Energy, Relearning and Owning attributes putting them into short phrases or "bullets".

Organizing them either by chronology or skills, the individual then considers the POV of the hiring manager and phrases "bullets" in her language. It may take more drafts to perfect the resume but the time is worth it.

Employment Interviews:

Here again the HERO method offers help to give the Hunter.

- As noted in the earlier ways to use HERO, a great way to use the Method is to set aside several (four or five) points that you want to make that your understanding of the employer POV directs you to make.

Set aside the points you want to emphasize and interject them into the conversation especially when facing the three main questions of the interview:

- Why do you want to work for me - what makes THIS place special to YOU?

- Why should I select YOU over the other applicants before me?

- Tell me about yourself - what makes YOU especially qualified for this job?

The Difference Between Sizzle and Steak

Version One:

"Mirage" Hickey sits impatiently while people hover around her, smearing acrylates copolymers, salicylic acid, octyl propenamide copolymers and alpha hydoxyl acids on her face while others aim a machine that blows *scalding* hot air at her head. She then walks to her job where strangers shout and grab at her legs and hands.

Version Two:

Beautiful Mariah Carey gets the royal treatment of top makeup artists and their *colorful* wares, while stylists prepare her *soft* hair for the *roaring* crowds at her latest sell-out concert.

I am describing the same reality, Mariah getting prepared for a concert, but one is the nitty gritty (the steak) and the other is the **excitement** you can related to (the sizzle).

In describing **your** experience and skills, make certain to talk of the *sizzle* using words they can relate to and paint a word picture of how their life will be easier with you as an employee:
** the customers will be happier
** work will get done without worry
** you will be reliable and fun to work alongside
** the employer's boss will be glad he hired such a gem.

You can see how this goes- - Burger places do not focus on telling you how cows are raised for their burgers, instead telling you how great they taste and how you will love them once you give them a try. Even eating more fiber (that tastes like cardboard) is good because it will make your body trimmer and sexier. **How do you sell *your* sizzle?**

Making It Work:

When employers ask you to "tell me about yourself" express why YOU R background meets what the employer needs. Make sure your ***"commercial"*** describes your skills.

Use examples how your Heart, Energy, ability to Re-Learn and how you Own your work helps
- make the *customers better*
- the company *reach its objectives* and
- make the *employer's life easier.*

You need to see this future before you can describe it and have the employer see it.

Write 8 sensory images and as many examples as you can of how you are the person for the job. (Seeing, touching, tasting, hearing and touching) Write the points you want to express below.

----

3 questions

In all of the interviews there are three basic questions that are either asked directly or indirectly and your being ready for them will put you ahead of the people who are not ready.

Tell me about yourself...

Connect what makes you special to the demands of the open job. Talk first of all that makes you different from other applicants and how that difference makes you a good fit for the job.

Be brief and focused in this question because rambling on about unrelated things will make the employer's mind wander **and when they wander, they normally wander away from you.**

Why should I hire you?

This is where you can make an image of your working there and to transfer that image to the employer's mind. Take all of the reasons you have why hiring you is a good idea and boil them down into a few central points.

You are showing how you are a better selection than others who may also be interviewed and that you have the essential ingredients for the job at hand.

HERO Method Workbook

<u>Why do you want to work for me?</u>

The employer is really asking "hey, we have some tough pressures on us. Do you know what you are getting into and will you have what it takes to stay here?"

The related question is "hey, if I hire you I am going to invest a lot of time, energy and personal pride in you - - are you going to stick around?"

Making It Work:

List the three questions then list as many ideas as you can to address each of them.

Next step, consider your top four prospective employers and put a number (1 through 4 for the employers) by each idea listed above and connect them to each employer keeping in mind the POV of each employer.

Have four points to make in answering each question and practice saying them aloud hearing how they sound and have the ring of being 'you'.

The "Janitor" Game

In order to express fully your qualifications, know

that just stating the title of a job you have held does not explain well what you have actually done.

Making a list of what you have done and listing them **from the new employer's point of view (POV)** - that is the only one that really matters – sets you apart.

Making It Work:

Write a list of the jobs/responsibilities you have done related to the kind of work you are looking into. For example, if you have worked extra hours when asked, completed training or helped others with training them, as that to your list.

Review the type of work you have done as if the person you are describing it to has **never** done that work before. If you cared for elderly patients, did you take vital signs? What do you mean by helping with hygiene? Did you ever work with groups of people? Make this part of the list as extensive as you can.

Once that list is completed, review it for each employer you are hoping to work for. Different employers will look at your experience differently, so mark up the different aspects of your experiences keeping in mind their POV.

In the end it is THAT POV that lands you the job.

The care and feeding of references:

Most hunters go about getting and maintaining references in the wrong way and the cost can be losing a job. You need to keep in touch with them and treat them for what they really are - an essential part of your upcoming success.

1. Make sure that the reference remembers who you are: When an employer calls references make sure that they do not turn into an owl. The employer calls and it just says "who? Who?"

Avoid your references from turning into an owl by keeping in regular contact with them and expressing your thanks to them for their time.

2. Make sure you don't have a school of fish for references. Many employers will only give the date of your hire and termination, sounding like a fish going "bluub, blub, blub".

Many employers will only give dates of your employment with no word of how you did. Make sure to learn if your references will do that and find other references who will not just say "blub, blub" to your next employer.

3. Another benefit of having your references

seeing themselves as appreciated and part of your success, they will not turn into a bear. Imagine a prospective employer calling someone who does not know you have them as a reference and they respond with "grrrr" angry that their time is taken up with something unexpected.

4. Often you will look for different jobs that are not directly related to the work or experience you have had with your reference. In that case, the prospective employer would ask "do you think this person would work well at my agency?" Unless the reference has had time to think it over, asked if you would be a good fit for the new job the he may turn into a dog and say "it would be rough, rough, rough".

With more thought, the reference may even turn to a sheep and say"baaad, baaaad".

Avoid this by reviewing with references examples of what you have done that warrant their support and keep them up to date on what kinds of jobs you are applying for.

To review:

* Do NOT ask if you can USE them as a reference - nobody likes to feel "used". Treat each person as being part of your future success.

Talk of the direction you are going and how they may be able to help you reach those goals. Remember that people love to participate in something bigger than themselves.

* Discuss with each reference something that makes you worthy of their support - something you have done to make them proud to be on your team. Try to make it connected to the kind of work you are looking for (see HERO Method).

* Always express thanks for their time and support with a call, a note or something that says each is appreciated.

6. Job Search pointers and misc.

Job hunting is one of the most frustrating things anyone will be doing throughout a lifetime. It relates to a person's sense of productivity, dreams for a future different from today, to the basics of how do I pay the rent next month?

In your work with the hunter to survive and thrive in looking for work, teach ways to stay motivated and positive in the longer days of the hunt. One way to help maintain the focus is to build a bullseye.

Building Your Own Bullseye

Wow! Days can be *long* out there job hunting. The deeply discouraging part is that each day in the hunt can seem *all-or-nothing.* Friends and relatives say "did you get the job yet?" (sounds like finger nails on a chalkboard, doesn't it?) or that neighbor **Jack** who twists his lip saying "so you still aren't working yet, ehhh?"

*You're putting in the hard work and hours of making contacts, but still you have to face **Jack** –*

Right now you have a tiny target that has only this itty-bitty bullseye labeled "got the job". Miss that target and you feel like a failure.

Here is a way to know you are moving forward even on days you don't land the job: *Folks, let's just make a bigger target!*

*Landing a job is really a series of steps where you progressively **move toward** that goal of the job. Let us make a target with that fact in mind.*

__Making It Work:__

Make a big bullseye covering 1 piece of paper with the center ring saying: "Got the job". **Now make** *several concentric rings around it, labeling each a step closer to the "Got the Job" goal.*

Examples include ** Listing potential employers ** finding name(s) of **person(s)** at the company who can offer job ** getting past the company 'bulldog' ** meeting or writing to the **person(s)** ** building a resume tailored to that job

Now make a list of **your** *top employers, giving each its own bullseye with concentric circles and succeeding chores. Put an "x" (and date it) where you currently stand with each employer and write below it what your next step will be to move closer* *to that bullseye.*

Make plans *each day* (written plans are best) on moving toward the target center with your employers, noting your *progress* with new x's (with dates) put on the targets as you move closer to the bullseye.

And smile when you see **Jack**, knowing even if you didn't hit the bullseye today, you hit the target and are *moving closer day by day*.

When building a bullseye is helpful but not enough, the job hunter needs to know that the efforts made are leading somewhere.

The day may not seem to bear fruit you can see - like a job offer or the chance to get a second interview - but something IS there in moving to that brighter future. You can teach that by learning from a lumberjack.

Learning From A Lumberjack

One of the most frustrating chores that I have done is chopping firewood. You swing the axe and maybe only chip off a little wood or sometimes nothing at all. It is frustrating and aggravating because on the outside all of that effort seems to be going nowhere.

How about friends who ask "how is the job hunt going, eh?" and for you the time is ticking by and **Nothing Is Happening**. Lots of effort, different swings and still not much happens. And the frustration you feel by the comments of others and the feeling that time is just ticking away.

The good news - there IS something happening with each swing. Inside that slab of wood, things ARE happening- bonds are breaking and what looks like something you will never crack is gradually breaking free. On the outside, the wood cutter is getting stronger, more determined and is one swing closer to your goal.

Again, it's that way in the job hunt. Each swing you make (interview, handshake, phone call) may not yield the visible results you want but each loosens what you may not be able to see:

- Another employer has heard about you.

- You have had another experience of connecting your skills to another job

- Another person knows that you are out there

and ready to work.

And things are also moving on the outside:

- You have practiced your stride, your "commercial" again

- You are picturing yourself working, making the image stronger with practice

- You are one swing closer to your goal.

Making It Work:

Make a list of all the different chores in the job hunt...

- making a list of prospective employers -finding the name of the hiring manager at each employer - using ways to contact that person.

Now make daily and weekly goals and know that you will make them and move forward toward your dreams even when you cannot directly see it.

Some parting thoughts:

In order to meet and defeat the challenges you are facing, **you need to practice** what you have learned before you go out to meet the employers. First of all, *practice* what you are going to say. Do not take my word for it; consider the story of:

Stan and Bruno, the talking dog:

Stan was a man down on his luck and with little money, sitting quietly with his dog Bruno in a park at favorite bench near the river. Stan sighed and idly asked his dog what he wanted to do.   To his surprise the dog said "I bet you'd like to take a swim. Hey, I'd like to join you."

Stan just stared as the silence between them grew. The dog spoke again "Hey, those Yankees are doing pretty well, huh? They have a great coach."

"Bruno! You can talk! We're going to be rich!! A talking dog, yahoo! We're going to that talent agent downtown right now!"

Bruno said, **"Hey, Stan, we should practice what we are going to say!"**

Stan said "no time to waste, we'll just start talking – it will be great!"

They reached the office building with a huge sign reading "Cash in on your talent" on top, then walked down the long hallway of photos of stars and into the talent agent's office.

The agent said "this better be good, most animal acts are not worth my time. "

Stan: "No problem. Hey Bruno, what is on top of this building?"

Bruno: "Roof! Roof!" **The agent just stared.**

Stan: "Let's... let's try this one – Bruno. Tell her about the hard times we have had, me without a job…" Bruno: "Rough, rough". The agent said "One last chance or I throw you out."

Stan: "OK, OK, Bruno… you're a big baseball fan, you love the Yankees, right? Who is the greatest Yankee ballplayer of all time?"

Bruno smiled and proudly said "Ruth, Ruth!"

The agent kicked them out of her office. Stan and Bruno sadly walked back to their bench. Bruno looked sadly at Stan and said "**We really should have practiced.** And I probably should have said Joe DiMaggio."

Folks, **don't be like Stan** – listen to your inner Bruno and always **practice aloud** the answers you may bring to an interview.

The hunter is having trouble getting to meet the hiring

manager? This is your opportunity to teach them about how to get past the gatekeepers who protect the hiring manager, the person I call the Bulldog.

Beating The Bulldog

You have reached a point in your hunt wherein know that hiring you is a good idea and you are looking for an employer who is smart enough to hire you. **But first you have to get past the "bulldog" staff standing between you and a chance to meet the employer.** But how can you do that?

She stands there, guarding her turf. And you are going to get past HER? HAH! Many have tried & failed, *slinking back home*, unable to get past her and get to that goal of so many others before have failed to do ... to meet the employer.

A "bulldog" is very good at guarding the employers time and keeping possible employees away by remembering a bulldog's two rules:

- The boss doesn't want to be disturbed, so don't waste his time with bad applicants.
- **Never forget rule number one.**

A bulldog needs to know whoever gets past her must be worthy of the employers time and attention. If she lets the wrong person by, the boss will remember her mistake long after the boss has forgotten the name of the bad applicant.

How will YOU get by?

By out-thinking the rules of bulldog-nicity.

1. Be politely insistent: Practice your cheeseburger voice & be genuinely polite, respecting the valuable time of both bulldog and employer. This can be a refreshing change from the others busy trying to see the boss.

2. Practice saying "that's OK, I'll wait" to

bulldog-isms like: "She's in a meeting, a long meeting" or "we are not hiring at the moment" or "we close for business in half an hour".

3. The dog may not know if there *is actually* an opening at the present time, but just using the line 'we're not hiring' to get you to leave. That's when your 'that's OK, I just want to shake her hand' works well.

4. Get an informational interview. Here you do not apply for a specific job, you only want to hear the employer's opinion on what kind of person he/she is looking for or info about the employer you can't get in the traditional ways. It works because as the saying goes, for many people there is no sound quite so sweet as the sound of their own opinion!

5. Get creative: One candidate stated in a letter that if I have not heard from you by Tuesday at 9 AM I will call then, then called saying the employer is expecting my call.

Make sure your creativity shows respect for their precious time, for their position and that this agency is special to you.

Making It Work:

THIS is a skill you can best develop through practice. Take the list you have of the employers you hope to work for and note next to them the name of a company bulldog you will meet. Maybe even greet the bulldog by name in the future.

With practice and time note how you were able to get past the bulldog to finally meet the employer. Practice (and success) will help build your skills.

Spirit

In all of the books I have read on job hunting, few discuss the spiritual side of the search. I do not mean this as a religious matter – just how you will be keeping your spirit and motivation 'up' while in the Hunt. Remember to take time for yourself and to appreciate the beauty around you. For example that you:

- See the beauty in things not necessarily man-made, but things like sunsets or the beauty in the night sky.

- Find a safe place where you can focus on the things important to you.

- **Put together a box that is all yours with things that give you a sense of peace – photos, things you enjoy doing, scents that you like.**

- List traditions that bring you peace of mind (such as saying thanks daily or playing favorite music).

Getting and keeping that feeling of being centered is like learning to ride a bike. Before you can move forward with confidence, you need to feel sure of your balance. Taking care of your 'spirit' will aid in getting that 'balance'.

Making It Work:

Here is something that can help you through the hunt – and often it is free. *Build a centering box –* put in a box or in the bottom of your sock drawer where you can.

Keep things in a box or drawer the items and images that help you feel more centered and at peace. Write down a list of what goes into that box.

Appreciate nature every day. Find something in the world around you that has its own rhythm (from the last song of the birds before sunset to the rattle of a passing subway car). Write a list of these things - - add to this list as days go by.

Write a list of traditions you have enjoyed that give you a sense of warming your spirit.

Spirit 2

As mentioned earlier, it is important to keep your spirit up as you face the challenges of job hunting. Remember to feel a sense *of gratitude in the gifts that you have* – the gifts of the world around you and the gifts that you have to share with others. It can make a lasting effect on you to make an inventory of what you need to support your personal spirit.

For example, building your HERO skills and your spirit can include helping others toward their goals. From helping someone with homework to joining a job hunting support group, you can feed your spirit in a special way.

Making It Work:

Let us address three-

- Gain a feeling of gratitude for the gifts you have by making an inventory of these gifts. Take a moment and list **gifts that you share with others** - - the sunshine, quiet times, 24 hours in a day and hope for the future for example.

Include the gifts of your physical body, intellect, your heart and ability to connect with others, your spiritual gifts of faith in yourself, others or your tomorrows.

- Make a list of the gifts you have received through the years - the people who have made an impression on your life; the opportunities (whether taken or not) to make a better life; the resources you have now to meet your daily needs. Think of ways to express your thanks for the gifts.
- Help others toward their goals – give them the benefit of your experience, expertise and caring. This helps open things in your life that only come out in caring for others. At the end of the day you will gain a sense that someone else's life is different because you were in it whether giving of your time, your

talents, or just a note to wish them well.

Partner Up:

There is an old Texas expression **that any mule can knock a building down, but it takes a good man or woman to build one up**.

Now that you have gone through these lessons, help other people to build that special future for them. In helping others you are able to better understand and put into practice what you know in job hunting for yourself and you will also get that priceless feeling that someone else's life is better because of your words and actions.

Also, make sure to thank the people who help you along the way. They have been seeing something in you maybe even before you saw it in yourself. Honor that with a thank you. They were your hero all along.

Congratulations on completing this book and good luck in the future.

<u>*Workshop 1.*</u> *My Inventory*

List below the things you have done <u>outside of work and family</u> – clubs, sports, volunteering

First column: A title for what I did

Second column: Describe what I did (duties, actions)

Third column: What I gained from it (skills, experience)

Fourth column: Full range of my responsibilities

Now do the same for your <u>Work Experience</u>: List every example of when there was something I did where I was given responsibility and I "did right by someone else" (from babysitting to volunteering work.

First column: A title for what I did

Second column: Describe what I did (duties, actions)

Third column: What I gained from it (skills, experience)

Fourth column: Full range of my responsibilities

HERO Method Workbook

Education and Training: Things I learned to be good (proficient) at, whether in school, at a job or in meeting personal and family needs.

First Column: Area of learning

Second Column: Benefit to me

Third Column: What I did with the learning

Fourth Column: How I know I am good at it

Workshop 2. My HERO qualities:

HEART: Work and life experience.

In column 1: Where I was:

In second column: People I worked with or helped:

In third column: Objective of that work:

People I served: Who they were/are
(characteristics – what is a common theme among
the people who were clients?)
:_____

What were/are they expecting from you? (the
client's objectives and perspectives):

_____

Was/Is the relationship to the client variable from
person to person? Give examples.

_____

Co Workers:

Who they are (experience, education, job
description):

_____

What are **they** expecting from **you** (getting along,
independent thought, etc.)

Is there stress/tension expected in your relationship (how to handle that):

Stakeholders of the employer: People who have a 'stake' in the operation of the employer – neighbors, media, etc.

Who are they? (Describe):

What do they expect from you?

Can you see the world from their POV?

General Issues:

Now we begin to see the world from a new employer's point of view. Select a prospective employer of interest to the job hunter and review THESE questions.

For each employer, review these questions.

Employer Point Of View:

Customers:

What kinds of problems or conflicts can you expect

to have on the job?

_____

Have you dealt with these kinds of conflicts or problems before and how well did you do with them?

_____

Co Workers:

What kinds of problems or conflicts can you expect to have on the job?

_____

Have you dealt with these kinds of conflicts or problems before and how well did you do with them?

_____

Stakeholders:

What kinds of problems or conflicts can you expect to have on the job?

_____

Have you dealt with these kinds of conflicts or problems before and how well did you do with them?

_____

ENERGY: Work and life experience.

In the first column:

Where I was/ my role in the work:

In the second column:

Examples of energy needed

In the third column:

Objective of that work/ outcomes:

Energy:

Here we continue focusing on a new job and the challenges ahead.

Employer Point Of View:

I want someone who faces challenges head-on.

Give examples of how/when you worked to resolve 3 tough problems:

I want someone who has worked hard when it was not expected, like overtime, or on a team practicing in the rain, something like that. Give me two examples of this you have done.

95

Everyone "hits the wall" and cannot work any further. Give an example of what it takes to exhaust you (this shows you understand your limitations):

_____

_____

I like people who volunteer and help out when they do not have to. Give me two examples of your doing this.

_____

RE-LEARNING: Work and life experience.

Re-learning is the ability of the individual to learn something efficiently and effectively so that they can be trusted to do it right.

In column one:

Name of position held

In column 2:

What I had to know to do the job

In column 3:

How quickly did I learn/ adapt

In column 4:

Special aspects (did I train others, etc.)

Employer Point Of View:

Training is one of the hardest parts of doing the job - things are always changing - and everyone says they can learn. Give three examples of something you had to learn well quickly and well.

_____

How did you KNOW you learned it, what gave you the understanding that 'yes, I have learned it well'?

_____

I need people who can adapt to change. Tell me three times when you adapted well the changes at work or school or life?

_____

Owning It: Work and life experience.

This section refers to taking responsibility for work by being conscientious, improving through the constructive criticism of others and being honest. This often is the hardest one part of HERO to put into action with the employer but also one of the most important.

First, review your work and personal history as it relates to Owning It. First go over the times you met stressful situations and came out stronger.

In the first column:

Description of experience

In the second column:

What made it hard/ stressful?

In the third column:

Specifics about the experience

In the fourth column:

How did you learn from it?

Employer Point Of View:

I want to find someone from this pile of applications who will make mistakes - everybody makes mistakes - then learn from them.

Give me examples of times you have messed up and later learned from the mistakes:

_____

It is rare to find people who welcome a challenge and are willing to say "yes, that one is for me." It is part drive, part learning from mistakes but all about being truthful with me instead of a lie. Give me 2 examples of you doing the right thing when taking another road is available:

Workshop 3.

The top four job prospects:

Listing the top four jobs I am hunting: (Repeated for each job)

First Job: Name of employer

_____

Name of job title I am hunting

_____

Heart:

As the employer, I need to know you will appreciate the needs and expectations of my clients. When you join my team, will you fit in or cause more trouble and make me regret hiring you?

The **clients or consumers** I will be dealing with in the job, what are they like?

_____

What do they want me to do for them/what do they expect of me in my new job?

_____

What is an example of a difficult situation I may be in with clients and how would I handle that?

Co-workers: How do they interact with each other and what will they expect from me?

Do we work together toward a goal or more individually? Do we face deadlines/pressure?

What is an example of a difficult situation I may be in with my coworkers - how to solve it?

Give 3 examples of the co-workers and management points of view in situations at work?

Stakeholders: Name three of them and describe how would I interact with them?

Energy:

Every job requires a level of energy - can you work as hard on days when it is sunny and you feel good as on rainy days when you wish you were home?

On a 'good day' at work, what are the physical and emotional challenges I will face?

On a 'bad day' at work, what are the physical and emotional challenges I will face?

_____

Re-learning:

I need to know that you can learn the work of the new job effectively and efficiently so I can walk away knowing the job will be done well. Can YOU do THAT?

What will I have to learn to meet the responsibilities of the job well? (Are they about dealing with "things" like numbers or machines or people?)

_____

Does the job require being quickness in doing the job well? Give three examples:

_____

Is there frequent training as systems change? Can I adjust?

_____

How will I know I have learned the job well and can do it effectively and efficiently?

_____

Owning the Job:

As the employer, I need to know that people will be

responsible for the work they do, good and bad. I need to know you will defend my company and its consumers the best you can.

Give three examples of being able to accept and learn from correction and criticism.

_____

Employers care for the quality of work completed. Give three examples of meeting responsibilities you have had and meeting another's expectations.

_____

In detail, what describe the worst parts of the new job. How will you handle it?

_____

You will need to defend our reputation to our clients. Can you handle the requirements of confidentiality and consistent customer service related to this job?

_____

Index IV: *Connecting the Dots:*

Putting it into words

Through the HERO Method, your role in the job hunt is partly helping the Hunter become motivated and more self-assured and partly helping her in understanding the employer's point of view and putting that knowledge into practice.

The final ingredient is learning how to put into words the connection between what the employer needs and what the Hunter can provide. The three main resources a job hunter has are resumes, applications and JIST cards. Here are ways to put these to the best use.

Here you can help the hunter put the connections into effective words. Here are some strategies:

Applications:

As you know, all an application needs to do is

1. get the employers attention, not get set aside into the pile of also-rans and

2. get the Hunter the opportunity for an interview.

Before writing anything on the application, look it over - this is the canvas you have the opportunity to paint your portrait on. Practice a bit and write five bullets indicating how your work and life experience meet what the employer needs. Write them down then check before writing on the application answer two questions

- does it use words appropriate to that employer?

- does it take into account the employer's point of view using HERO?

JIST:

JIST Cards are index sized cards which give job hunters the opportunity to put their qualifications together in short sentences or bullets form to highlight to the hiring manager why employing them is such a good idea.

The trick here is to focus on the wording the employer would appreciate. Make a rough draft from the study you have done regarding how your HERO skills relate to specific jobs.

Make certain you know the name, title and address of the hiring manager; write a cover letter then assemble one or two JIST cards specific to the job you are applying for and mail the person who can bring you closer to your dream.

Resume:

In building resumes which are specific to each prospective employer, the HERO Method gives the Hunter an opportunity to add personal experience as well as work history to the vitae.

By first approaching the resume from the employer's point of view and the HERO attributes she is looking for, the resume often writes itself. Make a list of the individual's Heart, Energy, Relearning and Owning attributes putting them into short phrases or "bullets".

Organizing them either by chronology or skills, the individual then considers the POV of the hiring manager and phrases "bullets" in her language. It may take more drafts to perfect the resume but the time is worth it.

Employment Interviews:

Here again the HERO method offers help to give the Hunter.

- As noted in the earlier ways to use HERO, a great way to use the Method is to set aside several (four or five) points that you want to make that your understanding of the employer POV directs you to make.

Set aside the points you want to emphasize and interject them into the conversation especially when facing the three main questions of the interview:

- Why do you want to work for me - what makes THIS place special to YOU?

- Why should I select YOU over the other applicants before me?

- Tell me about yourself - what makes YOU especially qualified for this job?

Index 5:

The range of your resources

There are ways of building up the qualifications you have in each area of the HERO Method. Help the Hunter appreciate she is in the process of becoming even more valuable to their next employer and through HERO she can focus on building further.

Heart:

You want to show that you can appreciate the needs, point of view and expectations of another person?

* Volunteer. Volunteer at a place wherein your work means something special to yourself. In this work you should seek to help individuals who have a perspective in life different from your own and maybe close to the point of view of the people you are hoping to work with in your new job.

* Get out and see the world from another person's viewpoint. Put yourself in a situation wherein someone expects something for you to do. Coaching or tutoring people will help give you this skill. Often a job shadowing experience in the field you are pursuing will help with that different perspective.

* If you are unable to volunteer with an agency, try helping neighbors who would appreciate your assistance. This gives you the opportunity to see the world from another's viewpoint and show that you care for another person's welfare.

For improving your skills in working as a teammate:

- Look into ways of helping in a team oriented event,

such as a local festival, project or event. This will give you the opportunity to show your community spirit and work alongside others toward a specific goal. Contact the local Chamber of Commerce for information on upcoming events you may join in.

- If you can offer a period longer than a day or two, look into joining a Board of Directors of an area human service agency you have strong interest in. Make certain that you do not select one that has a specific political leaning as this may turn off some employers.

In order to consider this further, get in touch with the administrators of these agencies and ask how you may help.

- Ask to "job shadow" in at a company or agency you may be interested in. This gives you valuable experience so you can understand directly the point of view of co-workers in the field. Career Centers or other programs to help job hunters can help you set up such an experience.

- If all of these options are out of your reach, try having an informational interview with someone in the line of work or at the employer you wish to be hired at. By meeting someone already in the field you will gain a better understanding of what the job and working at that new team will entail. Ask for a few moments of time and come armed with questions about the good and tough parts of the work day.

- Energy :

Show prospective employers you have energy and ability to meet the demands of the job:

* Challenge yourself! Write down a resolution that you would keep for yourself and self-improvement. Make the plan as specific and measurable as you can with a specific timetable that you can expect some success. Regular exercise is the best way to have focus on a goal that will give you a sense of accomplishment and improve your energy level.

* Challenge yourself by getting into community work in a way that challenges you. Think first of what a 'stretch' would be for you. Is it caring for an elderly person, writing a press release or selling tickets to an event? Ge out there and put some energy behind your choice.

* An essential part of HERO is developing the ability to see the world from another's point of view. Although it may not help in your job hunt directly, take time to write or call friends and family members thanking them for taking time to help you become the person you are. This helps you appreciate the energy and drive others have.

- Relearning:

* Take an adult learning class in your community as this shows your ongoing interest in learning. This will give you the opportunity to meet others in your interest maybe even build on your local contacts in the field.

* Thanks to the internet and on-line videos, you can learn the terms and their use in the field you are

considering entering quickly. One point of caution: Learning the words used in a field shows your interest and commitment to the field and may impress potential employers. First practice using them with people who know their correct useage as using them incorrectly is both funny and pretty darned embarassing.

* If you have the available time, an internship in the field you want to enter offers real-life experience in learning the sights, sounds and feelings related to a future job. It also offers a great reference valuable in the move toward your future.

* "MOOC", the nickname given to Massive Open Online Courses available for free on the internet, offers to you the opportunity to study in famous colleges and universities around the world. In these classes, you connect with students and instructors in a wide range of topic areas.

* There are dozens of learning websites where you can build your understanding and skills in a field you may feel you need help. Do you have difficulty in doing math? Look for sites that will help you brush up on this. Trouble fixing your car? There are dozens of sites and thousands of videos to help you here. Check into "do it yourself" sites, magazines or books so you can show to others - and to yourself - your ability to learn something new.

* This time can be an opportunity to learn a skill or enjoy a hobby. Make certain that what you do gives you the opportunity to learn something you appreciate and

can express some pride in your new understandings.

- Owning your work:

* One of the main benefits of building on ability to "own the work you do" is gaining a sense of self-confidence that you can grow from trying something new knowing that at the least, mistakes will help you grow. For example:

- Try something you may find scary, such as public speaking or assist in coaching a children's athletic team. - Put yourself in a position that may lead to condemnation, such as helping organize an event (try to avoid anything political in this work). - Learn something you have wanted to master but have been putting off, like playing a musical instrument.

* Think through times that you have learned from errors you have made. Make a list of examples and look for the 'common denominator' in them. Is there anything that connects the times when you made errors? Any way that has worked to help you learn from them?

People are often "creatures of habit" and these common connections may teach you insights that can help you in the future and show prospective employers that you have rare insight about yourself.

* Write to your family members or friends you have not been in touch with for a while. In your communication discuss old times together and any way related to resolve old conflicts.